Original By Design: The Brand Building Workbook

A brand so authentic, it sells itself

ORIGINAL

by

DESIGN

The Brand Building Workbook

Jaclynn Buchanan

Contents

How to Use This Workbook

This workbook is your personal companion to Original By Design. Each section mirrors a chapter in the book and gives you space to do the real work of building a brand that belongs entirely to you.

There are no wrong answers here. This is not a test. It is a discovery process. Some exercises will feel easy. Some will feel uncomfortable. The uncomfortable ones are usually the most important.

A few ground rules: Be honest. Nobody is grading this. Write the true answer, not the impressive one. Give yourself time. Do not rush through these pages in a single sitting. Come back to this workbook. Your answers will change as you grow.

At the back you will find a 30-Day Visibility Challenge and a Brand Audit you can return to every six months.

Jeremiah 29:11 says God has plans for you, plans to prosper you and not to harm you, plans to give you a hope and a future. This workbook is part of uncovering those plans. Take your time. Trust the process.

ADDITIONAL REFLECTIONS

Use this space for any additional thoughts, prayers, or ideas this section stirred up.

DETAIL 1

Discover Your Unique Talents

Your superpower is already within you.

Before answering, take a few deep breaths. These questions are not about who you think you should be. They are about who you already are.

Q1. What do people always come to you for, without you advertising it? What do they thank you for?

____

____

____

____

____

Q2. What activities make hours feel like minutes? When do you lose track of time completely?

____

____

____

____

Q3. What is something you do naturally that you have always assumed everyone can do?

____

____

____

____

Q4. What did you love doing as a child, before the world had opinions about it?

____

____

____

____

Q5. If money was never a factor again, what would you spend your time creating, teaching, or building?

____

____

____

____

Q6. What do people thank you for that you have been dismissing as just something you do?

____

____

____

____

Q7. Write a sentence that starts with: God gave me the gift of ______ so that I could ______.

____

____

____

____

Q8. What would change about how you show up if you fully believed your gifts were placed in you on purpose?

____

____

____

____

____

THE FIVE-PERSON EXERCISE

Reach out to five people who know you well and ask them: What do you think I am uniquely gifted at? What do you always come to me for?

Person 1

____

____

Person 2

____

____

Person 3

____

____

Person 4

____

____

Person 5

____

____

FINDING YOUR SWEET SPOT

Where do your passion, talent, and market demand overlap?

What I love doing (my passion):

____

____

What I am naturally great at (my talent):

____

____

What people need and will pay for (my market):

____

____

My Sweet Spot Statement: I help ___________ to ___________ by using my gift of ___________.

____

____

IF YOU ARE STARTING FROM ZERO

This section is for you if you picked up this book with a blank page, no following, no brand, not even a clear idea yet. Just a feeling. Answer these honestly.

Q1. If you strip away every expectation about what you should build, what is the one thing you genuinely feel pulled toward? It does not have to make sense yet.

____

____

____

____

____

Q2. What frustrates you most about the world around you? What do you keep wishing someone would fix, say, or create?

____

____

____

____

____

Q3. What do you already know, have experienced, or see clearly that could genuinely help someone else? You do not need credentials. You need honesty.

____

____

____

____

____

Q4. What would you build if you knew for certain that the right people would find it?

____

____

____

____

____

The blank page is not a problem. It is the most honest starting point there is. Write anything. Start somewhere. The brand will reveal itself as you go.

Jeremiah 29:11 says God has plans for you, plans to prosper you and not to harm you, plans to give you a hope and a future. You do not need to see the whole path. You just need to take the next step.

FROM GIFT TO BRAND: MAKING THE CONNECTION

You have identified your gift. Now let's build the bridge. These four questions are the skeleton of your brand. Answer them honestly and specifically, not how you think you should answer, but how it actually is for you right now.

Q1. What is the specific gift you identified in this section? Do not write a category. Write the actual thing.

____

____

____

____

Q2. Who is the one person who most needs what that gift produces? Not everyone. One person. Describe them in detail.

____

____

____

____

Q3. What changes for that person after they encounter what you build? What becomes possible for them that was not before?

____

____

____

____

____

Q4. Based on your answers above, write one sentence that describes what your brand exists to do. Gift plus person plus transformation.

____

____

____

____

This is your brand foundation. Everything else, the name, the content, the offers, the aesthetic, is just how this foundation shows up in the world. Come back to these answers whenever the building gets confusing.

Proverbs 18:16 says a person's gift opens doors for them and brings them before the great. The gift is what moves things. Your only job is to build something that lets the gift be seen.

DETAIL 2

Define Your Brand Identity

Become magnetic.

YOUR MISSION STATEMENT

A great mission statement answers: Who do you help, what do you help them do, and how?

Q1. Who do you most want to help? Be as specific as possible.

____

____

____

Q2. What is the transformation you want to create for them?

____

____

____

____

Q3. Why do you do this? What is the deeper reason behind it all?

____

____

____

____

My Mission Statement: I help ___________ to ___________ because ___________.

____

____

YOUR CORE VALUES

Check the values that feel most true to your brand. Then narrow to your top five.

☐ Authenticity

☐ Generosity

☐ Faith

☐ Excellence

☐ Joy

☐ Creativity

- [ ] Integrity
- [ ] Empowerment
- [ ] Courage
- [ ] Vulnerability
- [ ] Community
- [ ] Clarity
- [ ] Service
- [ ] Freedom
- [ ] Boldness
- [ ] Gratitude
- [ ] Growth
- [ ] Humor
- [ ] Wisdom
- [ ] Compassion

My top 5 brand values:

____

____

24

____

____

____

Q4. Choose one of your top values. How does it show up in your content and your work?

____

____

____

____

YOUR BRAND STORY

Q5. Where did you start? What is your before?

25

____

____

____

____

Q6. What challenge, doubt, or hard season did you face along the way?

____

____

____

____

Q7. What was the turning point? What shifted?

____

____

____

____

____

____

Q8. Where are you now, and how does your journey position you to help others?

____

____

____

____

____

____

____

YOUR VISUAL AND VERBAL IDENTITY

Q9. Write three words that describe your brand's tone of voice.

27

____

____

____

Q10. What content format feels most natural to you right now?

____

____

____

Q11. What do you want people to say about you when you are not in the room?

____

____

____

____

Q12. What would make someone choose you over anyone else who does something similar?

29

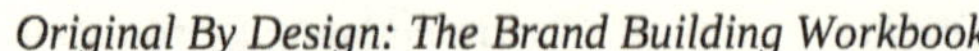

My goal was never to be liked by everyone. It was to see the gold in people and help them see it too.

DETAIL 3

Show Up and Own Your Space

Build trust and visibility.

Q1. What is the fear that most often stops you from showing up? Name it specifically.

____

____

____

____

Q2. What platform feels most natural to you right now? Why?

____

____

____

Q3. What does your ideal content look like? What topics would you cover?

____

____

____

____

____

____

YOUR VISIBILITY COMMITMENT

My primary platform:

____

I will post ___ times per week:

____

My content will focus on:

____

My posting schedule:

____

____

CONTENT IDEA BANK

Brain dump 20 content ideas right now. Do not filter. Just write.

1.

2.

3.

4.

5.

6.

7.

8.

9.

10.

11.

12.

13.

14.

15.

16.

17.

18.

19.

20.

Q4. What is one thing about your authentic self you have been afraid to share publicly?

____

____

____

____

____

Q5. Describe what showing up consistently looks like for you. Not the ideal version, the realistic one you can actually sustain.

____

____

____

____

____

Q6. What would you create or share this week if you knew no one was judging it?

____

____

____

____

Matthew 5:15 says you don't light a lamp and put it under a bowl. You put it on a stand so it gives light to everyone in the house. Visibility is not vanity. It is obedience to the calling God placed on your life.

ADDITIONAL REFLECTIONS

Use this space for any additional thoughts, prayers, or ideas this section stirred up.

DETAIL 4

Monetize Your Authentic Brand

Get paid for being you.

Q1. What belief do you have about money and your brand that might be holding you back?

____

____

____

____

Q2. Now challenge that belief. What would you say to a friend who told you that?

____

____

____

____

____

YOUR MONETIZATION OPTIONS

Check every method that excites you. Then circle your top two to focus on first.

☐   Digital products (e-books, templates)

☐ Online courses

☐ One-on-one coaching

☐ Group coaching programs

☐ Affiliate marketing

☐ Brand partnerships / sponsorships

☐ Speaking engagements

☐ Workshops and masterclasses

☐ Paid newsletter

☐ Membership community

☐ Consulting retainer

☐ Merchandise

Q3. Describe your first or next paid offering in detail. What is it, who is it for, and what would you charge?

____

____

____

____

____

____

Q4. What free value can you start giving right now that leads people toward that paid offering?

____

____

____

____

Q5. What would you charge if you truly valued your time and expertise? Write the number down.

Q6. Who is your ideal paying client or customer? Describe them in as much detail as possible.

YOUR REVENUE FUNNEL DRAFT

Free content (discovery):

Lead magnet (freebie to collect emails):

Nurture (how you stay in touch):

Offer (what you sell):

Revenue goal (6 months):

Deuteronomy 8:18 tells us God gives us the ability to produce wealth. Your gifts are not a coincidence. They are provision. You are allowed to prosper from them.

ADDITIONAL REFLECTIONS

Use this space for any additional thoughts, prayers, or ideas this section stirred up.

42

DETAIL 5

The Art of Adaptation

Stay true while evolving.

Q1. How has your brand or vision for it already changed since you first started thinking about it?

____

____

____

____

____

Q2. What is the core of your brand that you never want to change no matter what?

____

____

____

____

Q3. Where do you feel your brand is ready to grow or expand right now?

____

____

____

____

Q4. Is there something you have been holding onto out of fear of change rather than because it still serves you?

____

____

____

____

Q5. Think of a creator you admire who has evolved well. What did they keep? What did they let go of?

____

____

____

____

____

Q6. What is the next version of your brand calling you toward? Describe it even if it feels unclear.

45

____

____

____

____

____

YOUR BRAND ROOTS VS. BRANCHES

Roots: the non-negotiables that will not change. Branches: areas where you have room to grow.

ROOTS: things that will never change

____

____

____

____

____

BRANCHES: things I can evolve and experiment with

____

____

____

____

____

Philippians 1:6 says He who began a good work in you will carry it on to completion. Your brand is not finished. Neither are you. Trust the unfolding.

COMING BACK AFTER A GAP

This section is for anyone who had a brand, stepped away, and is now wondering if the door is still open. It is. Answer these at your own pace.

Q1. What pulled you away? Name it honestly without judgment. Life happens. This is just about understanding what the gap was.

____

____

____

____

____

Q2. What did the time away teach you, about yourself, your calling, or your brand, that you did not know before?

____

____

____

____

____

Q3. What felt most true about your brand before you stepped away? Is that still true? Has it deepened or shifted?

____

____

____

____

Q4. What is one honest thing you want to say to your community about where you have been? You do not owe anyone an explanation, but if you choose to share, what would feel true?

____

____

____

____

Q5. What is the smallest possible first step back? Not a full relaunch. Just one thing. What is it?

____

____

____

____

Isaiah 40:31 says those who wait on the Lord will renew their strength. The season away was not wasted. Come back renewed. Your people have been waiting for you.

ADDITIONAL REFLECTIONS

Use this space for any additional thoughts, prayers, or ideas this section stirred up.

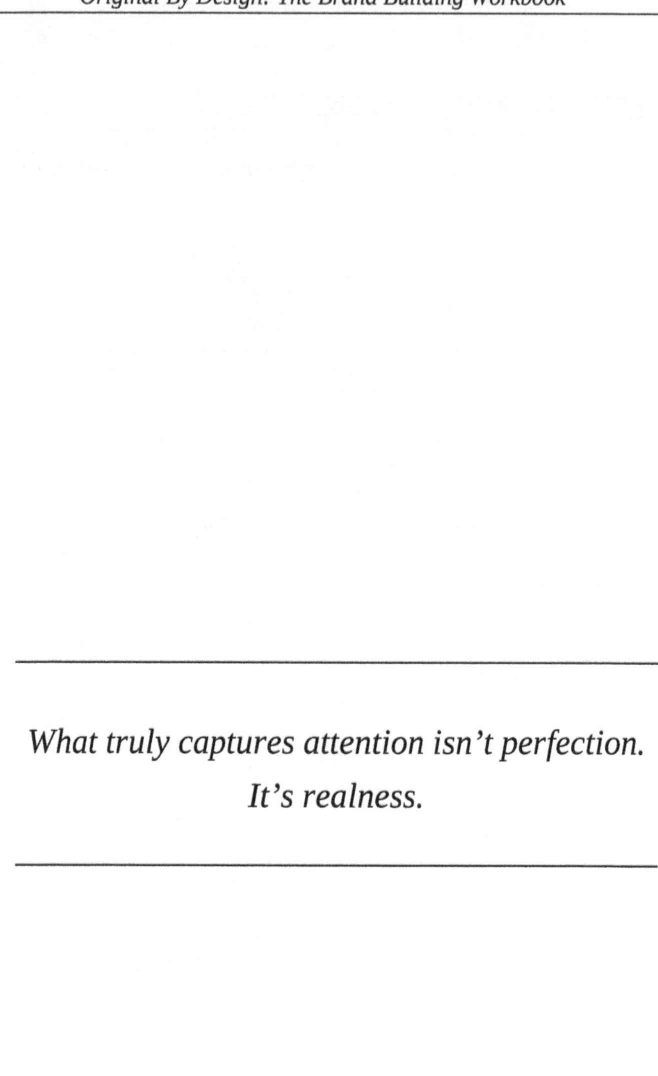

What truly captures attention isn't perfection.
It's realness.

There Is No Such Thing as Failure

It's all part of the story.

Q1. What is a moment in your brand journey that felt like failure? Describe it honestly.

____

____

____

____

____

____

Q2. What did that moment teach you?

____

____

____

____

Q3. Is there something you have been afraid to try because you are afraid of failing?

Q4. What would you do if you knew you could not fail?

Q5. Who has persisted through failure in a way that inspires you? What can you take from their story?

Q6. Write a letter to yourself from one year in the future, looking back at where you are now. What does that version of you say?

55

____

____

____

____

____

____

____

____

REFRAME YOUR SETBACKS

Think of three setbacks. In the right column, write what each one actually gave you.

Setback 1:

Setback 2:

Setback 3:

____

____

What it gave me:

____

____

Romans 8:28 says all things work together for good for those who love God and are called according to His purpose. Your setbacks are not wasted. They are working.

WHEN YOU WANT TO QUIT

Real talk. This section is not about motivation. It is about honesty. Answer these when you are in it, not after.

Q1. What is making you want to quit right now? Say the whole thing. Do not edit it for impressiveness.

____

____

____

____

____

Q2. Is this wanting to quit, or wanting a break? Be honest. They are not the same thing.

____

____

____

____

Q3. Go back to the reason you started. Not the strategy. The actual reason. Write it here.

____

____

____

____

____

Q4. Who in your life knows what you are building and actually believes in it? Have you talked to them lately?

____

____

____

____

Q5. What is the smallest possible next action, not the whole vision, just today? Write it down and do just that one thing.

____

____

____

Galatians 6:9 says do not grow weary in doing good, for at the proper time you will reap a harvest if you do not give up. The harvest is coming. Do not walk away from your field.

ADDITIONAL REFLECTIONS

Use this space for any additional thoughts, prayers, or ideas this section stirred up.

The Inner Work of Branding

What no one talks about.

Q1. Who do you most often compare yourself to? What does the comparison tell you about what you actually want?

____

____

____

____

____

____

Q2. What criticism has stayed with you? Write it out. Then ask: is this from someone in the arena, or the stands?

____

____

____

____

Q3. What is the story you tell yourself about why you are not ready yet?

____

____

____

____

Q4. If your brand were a person, how would you describe them?

____

____

____

____

Q5. What does the most secure, grounded version of you look like as a creator? Describe them.

____

____

____

____

____

____

Q6. What is one thing you would do differently in your brand if you were operating from confidence instead of fear?

____

____

____

____

IDENTITY CHECK-IN

Rate yourself honestly on each of the following from 1 (not at all) to 5 (completely). Circle your number.

I feel clear about who I am as a creator

1   2   3   4   5

I show up as myself, not a performance

1   2   3   4   5

I can receive criticism without it defining me

1   2   3   4   5

I celebrate other creators genuinely

1   2   3   4   5

I know my worth is not my metrics

1   2   3   4   5

I create from abundance, not fear

1   2   3   4   5

I have a support system around my building

1   2   3   4   5

I make time to fill my creative well

1   2   3   4   5

Q5. Which scored lowest? What is one small step you can take this week to strengthen it?

Psalm 139:14 says you are fearfully and wonderfully made. That is your identity. Not your follower count. Not your engagement rate. Build from that truth.

ADDITIONAL REFLECTIONS

Use this space for any additional thoughts, prayers, or ideas this section stirred up.

Q1. What do you want people to feel when they encounter your brand? Not think. Feel.

____

____

____

____

Q2. Describe your ideal community member in detail. Who are they? What are they hoping for?

____

____

____

____

Q3. What is one thing you can do this week to make a community member feel genuinely seen?

____

____

____

Q4. How do you currently engage with your audience? What is one way you could deepen that?

____

____

____

____

Q5. What would make someone feel so seen by your brand that they would tell a friend about it?

____

____

____

____

Q6. What kind of community do you ultimately want to build? Describe what it looks and feels like.

____

____

____

____

____

COMMUNITY BUILDING ACTION PLAN

Choose one action from each category to commit to this month.

One way I will make people feel seen:

____

One way I will create space for connection:

____

One community member I will spotlight:

____

One question I will ask my audience:

____

Hebrews 10:24 says to consider how we may spur one another on toward love and good deeds. Your brand can actually spur people on. That is not just a business outcome. That is a calling.

ADDITIONAL REFLECTIONS

Use this space for any additional thoughts, prayers, or ideas this section stirred up.

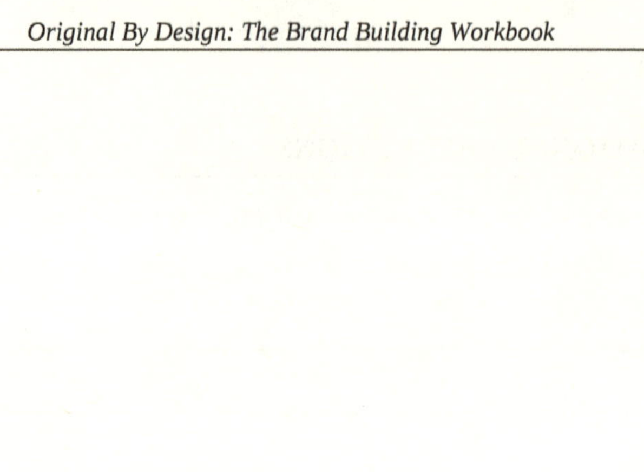
The biggest mistake you can make in building
your personal brand is hiding.

Collaboration Over Competition

Your so-called competition might be your greatest ally.

Q1. Who in your space do you genuinely admire? What do you admire about them?

____

____

____

____

Q2. Is there a creator you have been afraid to reach out to? Who and what is holding you back?

____

____

____

____

Q3. What could you offer to a potential collaborator? What makes your platform unique?

____

____

____

____

Q4. Is there someone in your space you have been treating as competition who could actually be an ally?

____

____

____

____

____

Q5. What would a dream collaboration look like for you? Who would it be with, what would you create, and who would it serve?

75

____

____

____

____

____

____

____

COLLABORATION WISHLIST

List five creators or brands you would love to collaborate with and one way you could add value.

1. Collaborator:

2. Collaborator:

3. Collaborator:

4. Collaborator:

5. Collaborator:

How I can add value:

Ecclesiastes 4:9 says two are better than one. You were not meant to build alone. Reach out to one person on that list this week.

ADDITIONAL REFLECTIONS

Use this space for any additional thoughts, prayers, or ideas this section stirred up.

> *You do not have to be the best at something to build something special from it. Just trust what God placed in you enough to actually use it.*

Managing Your Digital Footprint

Show up everywhere without burning out anywhere.

Q1. What is your home base platform right now? If you don't have one, which one feels most natural?

____

____

____

Q2. What are two or three outpost platforms where you can create lighter content?

____

____

____

Q3. Think of one piece of content you have. How could it be repurposed into three different formats?

____

____

____

____

____

____

CONTENT TIER PLAN

Long-form (deep authority content):

____

Medium-form (relationship content):

____

Short-form (discovery content):

____

Q4. What is your biggest challenge with staying consistent in your content?

____

____

____

____

Q5. What does your creative well need right now to keep flowing?

____

____

____

____

Q6. When you have burned out before, what was the warning sign you ignored? What will you watch for now?

____

____

____

____

Q7. What is one thing you could stop doing in your content right now that is draining you more than it is serving you?

82

____

____

____

____

____

____

____

ADDITIONAL REFLECTIONS

Use this space for any additional thoughts, prayers, or ideas this section stirred up.

> *A brand that stays stagnant risks becoming irrelevant. A brand that changes too much loses its soul. The art is in growing while staying rooted.*

DETAIL 10
Your Brand in Real Life

Personal branding happens offline too.

Q1. Think of someone who has met you in person. What do you think they walked away feeling about you?

____

____

____

____

Q2. Is the person you are online the same person you are offline? If there is a gap, what is it?

____

____

____

____

Q3. What in-person opportunities have you been avoiding or delaying?

____

____

____

____

Q4. What everyday experience from your life would make a powerful, authentic piece of content?

____

____

____

____

Q5. Think of the last time someone told you that you made an impression on them. What did they say, and what does that tell you about your brand?

87

____

____

____

____

Q6. How do you want people to feel after spending time with you, whether in person or online?

____

____

____

____

Q7. What is one in-person connection you have been putting off that you will commit to making in the next 30 days?

____

____

____

____

____

IN-PERSON BRAND GOALS

One event I will attend in the next 90 days:

____

One person I will follow up with this week:

____

One speaking opportunity I will pursue:

____

Isaiah 50:4 speaks of having an instructed tongue, to know the word that sustains the weary. Your voice, live and in person, carries a power that goes beyond content strategy. Use it.

ADDITIONAL REFLECTIONS

Use this space for any additional thoughts, prayers, or ideas this section stirred up.

Every so-called failure is just data dressed up in disappointment. Your only job is to learn from it and keep going.

Knowing When to Say No

Protecting your brand when the money is on the table.

Q1. Have you ever said yes to an opportunity that did not align with your brand? What happened?

____

____

____

____

____

Q2. What is the hardest type of opportunity for you to say no to, and why?

____

____

____

____

Q3. Write your personal brand alignment checklist. What questions will you always ask before saying yes?

____

____

____

____

____

____

____

Q4. What would you need to see, hear, or feel in an opportunity before saying yes with full confidence?

____

____

____

____

Q5. Is there a standing opportunity or commitment in your brand right now that you need to say no to? What is stopping you?

____

____

____

____

____

MY BRAND BOUNDARIES

Complete these statements clearly so you have them ready before the next opportunity arrives.

I will never promote or partner with:

____

I will only say yes to deals that:

____

The question I will always ask first:

____

When I feel pressured to say yes, I will:

____

Matthew 6:24 says you cannot serve two masters. Know who you serve and let that clarity guide every decision.

94

An audience follows your content. A community follows you. Build the kind of brand that makes people feel like they belong to something bigger than a content calendar.

Q1. In ten years, what do you want people to say about what you built? Write it as if someone is giving a speech.

____

____

____

____

____

____

Q2. Who is one person you can pour into or mentor right now?

____

____

____

____

Q3. What piece of content or work do you want to create that you believe could still help people in five years?

____

____

____

____

____

Q4. What does success feel like to you when you strip away the numbers?

____

____

____

____

Q5. What is one thing you want to have built, started, or set in motion in the next twelve months that moves you toward that legacy?

____

____

____

____

____

Q6. Who in your life right now could you pour into, mentor, or open a door for? What is one step you could take this week?

____

____

____

____

____

Q7. What is the one thing you want to be remembered for, above all else, in the work you do?

YOUR LEGACY STATEMENT

Write a first draft of your legacy statement. Not a mission statement. What do you want to have meant?

____

____

____

____

____

____

____

2 Timothy 4:7 says I have fought the good fight, I have finished the race, I have kept the faith. That is the legacy worth building toward. Not fame. Faithfulness.

ADDITIONAL REFLECTIONS

Use this space for any additional thoughts, prayers, or ideas this section stirred up.

ADDITIONAL REFLECTIONS

Use this space for any additional thoughts, prayers, or ideas this section stirred up.

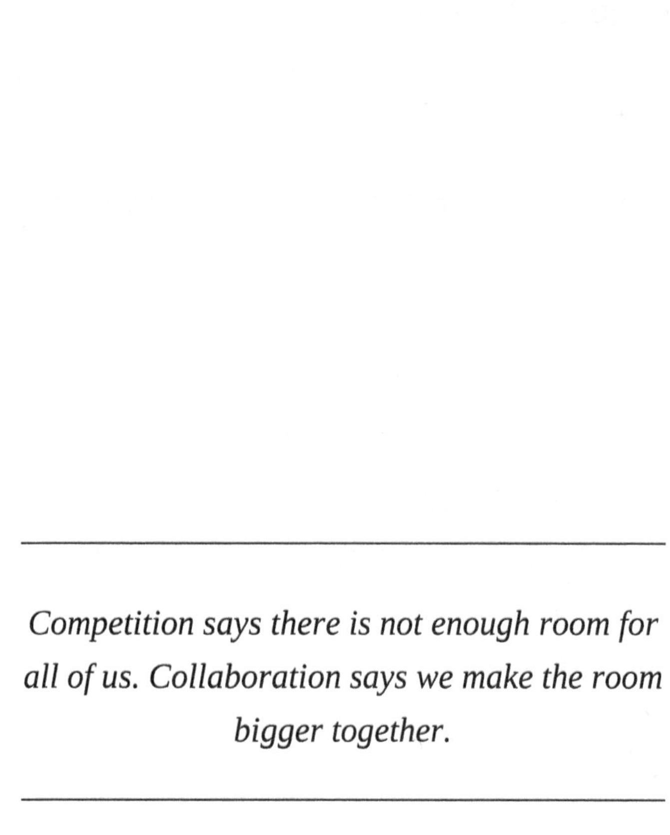

Competition says there is not enough room for all of us. Collaboration says we make the room bigger together.

Good Day Agency was built for creators who are done being told to chase trends, copy what is working for someone else, or water down their voice to fit a mold the market invented.

Q1. What is the most authentic version of your brand? Not the most marketable. The most true.

____

____

____

____

____

Q2. What would your brand look like if you stopped trying to appeal to everyone?

____

____

____

____

____

Q3. What trend or expectation have you been following that does not actually feel like you?

____

____

____

____

____

Q4. Where in your brand are you performing instead of being? What would it look like to drop the performance?

____

____

____

____

____

Q5. What calling or conviction keeps showing up for you that you have not fully acted on yet?

____

____

____

____

____

Q6. If your brand was built entirely from what God placed in you, with no concern for trends or approval, what would it look like?

____

____

____

____

____

____

____

YOUR AUTHENTIC BRAND DECLARATION

Write a declaration to yourself about who you are as a creator, right now, at your most honest.

____

____

____

____

____

____

____

____

____

John 8:32 says the truth will set you free. The most freeing thing you will ever do as a creator is decide to be fully, unapologetically yourself.

ADDITIONAL REFLECTIONS

Use this space for any additional thoughts, prayers, or ideas this section stirred up.

Your reputation is built in the spaces between the content. Who you are when no one is filming is the truest version of your brand.

30-Day Visibility Challenge

Show up every day for 30 days. Not perfectly. Just honestly.

This is the simplest and most powerful thing you can do right now: show up every day for thirty days. One piece of content. One story. One honest moment. It does not have to be long. It does not have to be polished. It just has to be real.

Platform I am committing to:

____

Start date:

____

My accountability partner:

____

DAILY TRACKER

Check each day as you complete it and write one word describing how it felt to show up.

☐ Day 01

☐ Day 02

☐ Day 03

☐ Day 04

☐ Day 05

☐ Day 06

☐ Day 07

☐ Day 08

☐ Day 09

☐ Day 10

☐ Day 11

☐ Day 12

☐ Day 13

☐ Day 14

☐ Day 15

☐ Day 16

☐ Day 17

☐ Day 18

☐ Day 19

☐ Day 20

☐ Day 21

☐ Day 22

☐ Day 23

☐ Day 24

☐ Day 25

☐ Day 26

☐ Day 27

☐ Day 28

☐   Day 29

☐   Day 30

Q1.   At the end of 30 days, reflect: What did you learn about yourself? What surprised you? What shifted?

____

____

____

____

____

Q2.   Which day was the hardest to show up? What got you through it?

____

____

____

____

Q3. What would you do differently in your next 30 days of showing up?

Every yes you give to something that does not fit is a no to something that does. Your time, your platform, and your audience's trust are not unlimited resources. Spend them wisely.

Set a reminder right now. Every six months, return to these pages and answer these questions honestly. Your answers will change. That means you are growing.

Date of this audit: _______________________________

Q1. Is my current content still a true reflection of who I am and what I stand for?

____

____

____

____

Q2. Am I serving my community well? What do they need from me right now?

____

____

____

____

Q3. What opportunities have I said yes to in the last six months that I should have said no to?

____

____

____

____

Q4. What have I been afraid to do or say in my brand that I need to finally do or say?

____

____

____

____

Q5. What is the single most important thing I want to build or accomplish in the next six months?

____

____

____

____

BRAND HEALTH SCORECARD

Rate each area from 1 (needs serious work) to 5 (thriving and strong). Circle your number.

Clarity of mission and message

1   2   3   4   5

Consistency of showing up

1   2   3   4   5

Authenticity of my content

1   2   3   4   5

Depth of community connection

1   2   3   4   5

Quality of collaborations and partnerships

1   2   3   4   5

Alignment of monetization with my values

1   2   3   4   5

Health of my creative energy

1   2   3   4   5

Confidence in saying no to misaligned opportunities

1   2   3   4   5

Building with legacy in mind, not just metrics

1   2   3   4   5

Overall: my brand feels like ME

1   2   3   4   5

Q6.   Which area scored lowest? What one specific thing will you do in the next 30 days to strengthen it?

Q7. Looking back at where you started, what growth are you most proud of in your brand so far?

____

____

____

____

____

____

Q8. What would you tell someone just starting out that you wish you had known when you began?

____

____

____

____

____

____

Q9. Write a commitment to yourself: I will honor the gifts God placed in me by doing _______ consistently, starting _______.

____

____

____

____

Lamentations 3:22-23 says God's mercies are new every morning. Every six months, every new season, every new chapter, you get a fresh start. Come back to this audit and let it remind you of how far you have come.

ADDITIONAL REFLECTIONS

Use this space for any additional thoughts, prayers, or ideas this section stirred up.

You did the work. Now go build it.

The world is waiting for the real, passionate, one-of-a-kind you.

Jaclynn Buchanan